THE STORY OF
KARATE

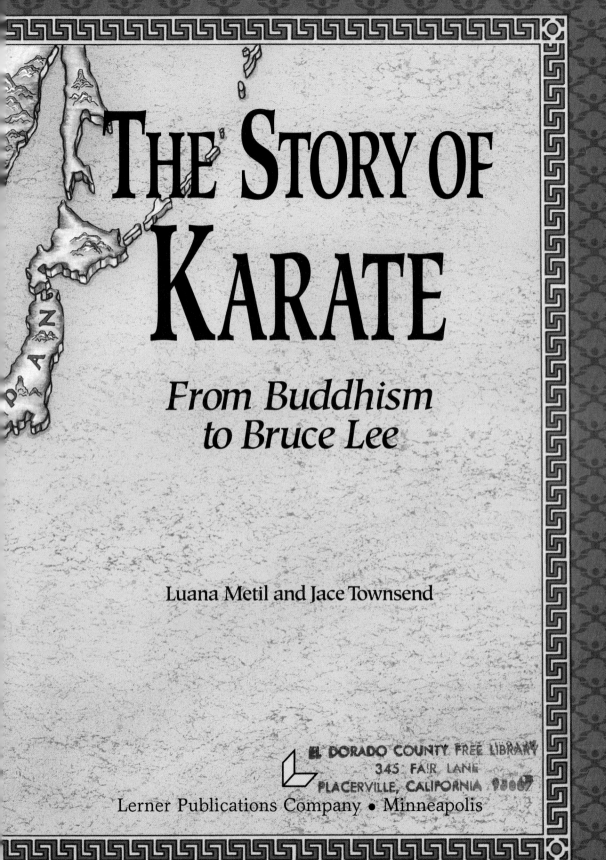

THE STORY OF
KARATE

From Buddhism
to Bruce Lee

Luana Metil and Jace Townsend

Lerner Publications Company • Minneapolis

For Jeffrey and Julia

Library of Congress Cataloging-in-Publication Data

Metil, Luana.
    The Story of Karate : from Buddhism to Bruce Lee / by Luana Metil and Jace Townsend.
        p. cm.
    Includes index and bibliographical references (p.).
    ISBN 0-8225-3326-1
    1. Karate–History–Juvenile literature. 2. Hand-to-hand fighting, Oriental—History—Juvenile Literature. [1. Karate–History. 2. Martial Arts–History.] I. Townsend, Jace. II. Title. III. Series.
    GV1114.3.M48   1994
    796.8'163—dc20
                                                                93-32006
                                                                    CIP
                                                                    AC
                                                                    Rev.

Manufactured in the United States of America

1 2 3 4 5 6 – I/JR – 00 99 98 97 96 95

Contents

INTRODUCTION

For as long as humans have existed, they have had to defend themselves—against the elements of nature, against wild animals, and against other people. The ways in which people defend themselves are as diverse as the people. While many defenses are instinctive and particular to the person and situation involved, other defensive styles have been adopted and modified by large groups of people. Karate is one such method.

Ancient paintings on tomb ceilings and carvings on temple walls show us that fighting arts have existed for thousands of years. Karate, which we now think of as a sport as well as a method of self-defense, has a rich and complex past. Karate is a system of unarmed fighting, using kicks and hand thrusts, that has been woven together from many countries, philosophies, and cultures. Each of the four major karate styles—Chinese kung fu, Okinawan karate, Korean tae kwon do, and Japanese karate—used specific techniques to fit its culture, geography, and resources.

Opposite page: Early legends told of superhuman feats performed by those skilled in the fighting arts.

This mural shows monks at the Shaolin Temple, practicing the martial arts.

One of karate's origins was in a temple, as a series of exercises for monks. Legends tell of a monk from India who taught a way of exercising as well as a way of religious living. Unraveling the mystery of karate's origins also shows a thread leading back to desperate Okinawan farmers, grasping their field tools to defend their farms against marauders. Yet another thread in karate's tapestry is the Japanese warrior way of life, based on a philosophy of harmony and strict moral behavior codes.

Kung fu fighters from southern China used low stances with both hands making circular motions. They needed low stances to keep their balance while fighting on boats and slippery muddy ground, common in that area. Using their strong arms and hands came naturally for them because they were farmers. Northern Chinese kung fu artists stood up straighter and used more kicks to knock attackers off horses. They could kick well because they had strong legs from walking up and down the steep hillsides of their region. The Japanese developed a style using straight paths for quick attack and retreat. The Okinawans moved in straight lines, but also used circular blocking movements as in kung fu. The Koreans added many high spinning kicks to their style.

During the twentieth century, the Asian fighting arts made their way through Europe and the Americas, again changing to fit the place and time. American karate is evolving from a combination of systems. All styles have great speed and devastating power. What style works best depends on the specific situation.

The complete history of the fighting, or martial, arts probably will remain a mystery forever. Much of the written history of karate was lost in fires and wars throughout the ages. There were also long periods of time when martial arts were only practiced in secret because they were feared and forbidden by ruling governments. Despite this, the legends live on through all those who practice these ancient arts today.

Karate students today practice in gymnasiums and recreation centers.

This soapstone figurine of Bodhidharma dates from the Ming-Qing Dynasty in the seventeenth or eighteenth century.

1

THE
LEGEND OF
BODHIDHARMA

Kings in India, ever since 1,000 B.C., had warriors to guard them and their temples. The warriors fought when necessary, and their job was so important that they spent most of their time practicing and perfecting new moves for battle.

In sixth century A.D., a young boy named Bodhidharma watched these warriors practicing their fighting skills. He enjoyed watching them move gracefully like dancers as they kicked and thrust punches at imaginary enemies. The warriors were called kshatriyas (sha-TREE-as) and they called their fighting art vajramushti (vah-ra-MOOS-ty).

Bodhidharma's family belonged to the kshatriyas warrior class and had many privileges. Bodhidharma had private tutors to educate him and free time to watch the warriors practicing their movements. He was a serious boy who deeply believed in his religion, Buddhism—the major religion in India and China. Buddhism teaches that good deeds done during life on earth will be rewarded in the next life, and wrong behavior will bring misfortune.

When Bodhidharma was grown, he became a Buddhist monk. He practiced his religion by sitting silently for long periods of time, an exercise that is called meditating. He believed people could find inner peace and holiness within themselves rather than through reading religious scriptures. Bodhidharma felt people should concentrate on the present moment, rather than thinking of the past or future.

Stone statues at the Shaolin Temple depict monks in meditation.

Monks often traveled between India and China, bringing Buddhist scriptures to the new temples in China. Bodhidharma decided to go to central China and visit a new Buddhist monastery, called the Shaolin (show-LIN) Temple. He traveled over rough seas, lonely plains, mountains, rivers, and dark forests for more than 2,000 miles to reach it. The long distance over rough and wild terrain made the trip physically difficult. Robbers along the way made the journey dangerous. Most merchants traveling at that time hired bodyguards for protection, and some monks learned ways to protect themselves.

Since Bodhidharma was from the privileged class, he was allowed to visit with the emperor of China on his way to the temple. What, the emperor is said to have asked Bodhidharma, will I get as a reward in the afterlife for having built the Shaolin Temple? Bodhidharma replied that he would receive nothing. To Bodhidharma, doing the deed was a reward in itself and nothing more was important. For Bodhidharma, rewards in another lifetime and the promise of worldly goods were not the way to blessedness, or nirvana, despite what other Buddhists taught.

——— *A New Religion Begins* ———

The Shaolin monks were excited to have Bodhidharma visit them because they felt he was a very special man. They had heard tales that he performed supernatural feats. Stories were told of Bodhidharma crossing a river by simply standing on a reed. But when Bodhidharma arrived at the temple, the head monk would not let him enter. He was afraid Bodhidharma's new religious ideas would disrupt his monastery, where the monks spent most of their time translating Indian scriptures into Chinese.

So, legend states, Bodhidharma sat in a nearby cave, staring at the wall in deep meditation for nine years. Bodhidharma was able to empty his mind and concentrate on the present moment so completely that, he said, he could even hear the ants on

A stone marker in the Shaolin Temple courtyard commemorates the temple's importance in martial arts history.

The Story of Karate

Bodhidharma's physical fitness enabled him to meditate for long periods.

the cave wall screaming! His concentration was so total that he was not even aware of birds nesting on his shoulders. When the head monk saw that Bodhidharma's eyes had pierced a gaping hole in the cave wall, he invited Bodhidharma into the temple. As the monks and others began to understand and accept Bodhidharma's beliefs, their new religion, Chan Buddhism (also known as Zen Buddhism), was born.

The Shaolin monks spent most of their time praying and writing about their religion. They did not get much exercise, which left them weak and flabby. Unlike Bodhidharma, the Chinese monks collapsed or fell asleep when they sat still for long periods. Their already weak legs became weaker. So Bodhidharma taught them the exercises he had learned from the vajramushti warriors in India. These movements and breathing techniques were the beginning of karate.

—— Harnessing the Life Force ——

The exercises, like Zen philosophy, helped the mind and body to work in harmony, together as one. For a person's mind to concentrate to its fullest, that person's body must be at its best. Bodhidharma taught the monks a way to breathe for inner calmness that helped them to sit quietly for long periods of time.

Stone statues in the courtyard of the Shaolin Temple illustrate the exercises Bodhidharma taught the monks.

Since ancient times, the Chinese have thought of the ch'i (chee) as the life force that exists in all living things. It is the internal energy that flows through the body. A person experienced in martial arts learns to control the ch'i.

The ch'i breath flows from the body's center of gravity, which is just below the navel. Slow, deep breathing, called ch'i breathing, helps those who practice it to control their feelings and thoughts so they can focus their minds and bodies on the present moment. Ch'i breathing also gave the monks the energy to stay awake while they sat meditating.

Stretching exercises kept the monks' muscles from cramping and their joints from getting stiff while they sat for many hours. Muscle-building exercises kept the Shaolin monks strong and physically fit, like Bodhidharma.

The graves of Shaolin monks are marked by stone sculptures.

The monks named Bodhidharma's exercises The Eighteen Hands of the Lo Han, meaning exercises for the ultimate—or greatest—holiness. They felt Bodhidharma had given them a great gift.

One legend claims that on the day of Bodhidharma's death, a man met a monk who claimed he was Bodhidharma on his way back to India. The man noticed the monk was wearing only one sandal. He told Bodhidharma's followers the story. When they opened his coffin, they found it empty—except for one sandal.

Paintings of ancient monks in martial arts poses adorn the walls of the Shaolin Temple's Hall of the Thousand Buddhas.

2

Shaolin Monks and Kung Fu

Several centuries after Bodhidharma's death, Shaolin monks were still practicing The Eighteen Hands of the Lo Han. These exercises were practiced for strength and general health, not for fighting. However, the monks needed to know how to defend themselves and their temple, which was in a remote area in the Songshan Mountains, far away from other people. Bandits were a threat to the monks when they traveled

The monks believed life was sacred and should be defended. They would never start a fight, but they would fight to save their lives and protect their temple. They created more exercises for self-defense and practiced punching, kicking, and blocking. They found that ch'i breathing, which helped them feel calm inside, also helped to increase their striking power. What had given them energy to pray also gave them energy to fight. When they breathed deeply and exhaled forcefully, their muscles tensed, and explosive strength went into each punch or kick.

Opposite page: Fierce-looking figures in martial arts poses guard the Shaolin Temple entrance.

Their exercises also were influenced by the philosophy of Lao Tzu, who lived in China in the sixth century B.C. He was a scholar who believed in living in harmony with nature and understanding the balance of opposites in the universe. This philosophy is known as Taoism (DOW-ism). The symbol of yin-yang represents the universal harmony created by the balance of opposites. The light side, called the yang, and the dark side, called the yin, are the

The yin-yang symbol, in the center of the scroll, represents the harmony of nature.

opposites that flow together into a perfect whole. Inside each is a small part of its opposite. The symbol represents the harmony of life, from the unity of heaven and earth to the harmony of mind and body working together.

——— Lessons from Nature ———

The monks felt it was important to live in harmony with nature. They respected all the animals around them. Long before Bodhidharma, a Chinese doctor named Hua To taught that imitating animal movements would improve general health. Much later, in the thirteenth century, two masters of Bodhidharma's Eighteen Hands, named Chueh Yuan and Li Cheng, spent many years watching animals. They studied all kinds of animals, from insects to large, wild cats. They learned animal stances and movements that they added to the exercises. Another monk, Pai Yu Feng, added more movements. Eventually the 18 exercises grew to 170 techniques.

The monks named several new exercise movements for the animals. They watched the tiny praying mantis patiently wait and conserve its energy until its opponent was close enough to be captured with one blow. So the monks practiced timing and speed until they could catch a buzzing fly with their chopsticks with one swipe through the air.

Snakes rapidly strike sensitive areas on their prey. The monks learned to strike sensitive areas to immediately take down or disarm an opponent. To strike exactly the right spot required pinpoint accuracy.

The monks practiced balancing on one leg, then the other, in the one-legged stance of the crane. Balance is important when making fast movements.

By quickly somersaulting and jumping about from side to side and back and forth, a monkey confuses its opponent. The opponent is left twirling about while trying to follow the monkey. Several of the Shaolin exercises imitate the low and rapid movements of a monkey.

A tiger uses its sharp claws and strong legs to

The crane stance is just one movement that martial artists have learned from observing animals.

strike with strength and speed. The monks practiced the tiger claw strike with curved fingers aimed at the attacker's face and eyes.

The monks practiced jumping kicks used by deer. They also practiced the strong and solid stance of a horse and its rider. In the horseback stance, the monk had his legs apart, knees bent, and was ready to hold his ground.

In addition to the many animal movements the monks practiced, they also wanted to possess the power of the mythical dragons in the Chinese culture. Dragons were thought to have enormous strength. When someone fought with the spirit of a dragon, they were said to have its amazing power. The dragon breathed out fire, and the monks imitated that when using the energizing ch'i breathing Bodhidharma had taught.

— A Way of Life —

The Shaolin monks eventually developed a complete fighting style for self-defense. In China it is called wu shu (woo SHOO), or Shaolin Temple boxing. In Western countries, it is known as kung fu (kung FOO). The monks devoted their lives to the perfection of kung fu philosophy and skills. Each monk tried to live with his mind and body working together in harmony. Kung fu was spiritual as well as physical. It was a way of life, not just a way of fighting.

Some monks were experts in Chinese traditional medicine. They understood the human body and knew its weakest, most sensitive spots. They knew how to stun, or even kill, a human by applying

The Shaolin monks developed their exercise routine into a martial arts form, which is called kung fu in Western countries.

The Shaolin monks could fight off bandits so effectively that stories of their great fighting skills spread throughout China.

pressure to one of the 108 vital points on the body. With this knowledge, they learned how to stop an attacker by striking these spots, often bringing the opponent down with one well-aimed blow. With strength, skill, and spirit, they were a powerful force.

A famous legend of the Shaolin monks tells of their graduation ceremony. After years of training, the kung fu student completed his study with a final test. The student was sent alone into the temple's underground passageways and rooms.

The hallway was filled with spears pointing out from the walls, so one wrong or sudden turn could end his test and his life. The student had only his senses and instincts to be ready for whatever happened. On the wall of one room were several implements and a sign that read "choose one." When he entered the next chamber, he was surrounded by scorpions. Using his chosen tool, he had to quickly get rid of the scorpions that had crawled on him and into his path. He was lucky if he had chosen the broom instead of the sword; then he could sweep them out of his way. In another room, an avalanche of rocks fell. If he could quickly dodge the rocks, he would not be crushed.

To open the final door, the student had to move a large cauldron filled with boiling water. On each side of the cauldron was the raised design of a dragon. The only way to move the cauldron from the doorway was to lift it with his bare hands and arms. His flesh burned as he grabbed the cauldron. When he opened the door to the world outside, he had his diploma—the cauldron's dragons permanently scarred onto his arms.

Monks' Fame Spreads

The Shaolin monks could fight off bandits so quickly and effectively that stories of their great fighting skills spread throughout China. One legend describes a lone monk walking to visit a neighboring temple. The moon was hidden behind a cloud and a fine mist was in the air, making it impossible to see

clearly. The night was so quiet he could hear the faint evening breeze gently rustling the leaves. As he walked on, he heard the sound of creeping footsteps off to the side of the road. He felt someone's presence and sensed danger. He kept walking, but was ready to fight.

The bandits thought it would be easy to frighten and rob this man, who was alone. Quickly, they attacked. Two of them jumped in front of the monk as a third bandit attempted to grab him from behind. The monk sidestepped the bandits before they even touched him. The two in front lunged at the monk with knives, stabbing the air. For several minutes they twirled, swung, and kicked in the darkness, never making contact with the monk. Suddenly the monk gave a loud yell and kicked the legs out from under one bandit. Then he ducked down into a squat, twirled around, and sent the second one sprawling with a blow. The third bandit saw a tiger claw appear in his face as his arm was bent, forcing him to drop his knife.

It all happened so quickly that the bandits thought they had been kicked by a deer, chased by a monkey, and attacked by a fierce and snarling tiger. The monk was able to disarm and overpower them all so easily that they thought he must have really been several people and animals. They were amazed by his fighting ability and their stories quickly spread.

—— *Fighting for the Emperor* ——

Even the rulers of China asked the Shaolin monks to help fight their enemies. In A.D. 621, about a hundred years after Bodhidharma's visit, Prince Li Shimin was captured by General Wang's rebel army near the Shaolin Temple. The prince immediately sent word to the temple, asking the monks for help.

Martial arts history is depicted in a mural at a training center at the Shaolin Temple.

Shaolin Monks and Kung Fu

The Shaolin monks ambushed and chased away Wang's men, freeing Prince Li. When Prince Li was named emperor, he showed his appreciation by rewarding the fighting monks. A great banquet was held in their honor. Monk Tan Chung was given the title of Great General, while the temple was given much additional land and permission to keep a standing army of monk soldiers. One legend states that the monks also were allowed to wear gold-colored clothing, which previously had been reserved for the emperor. The emperor even invited the fighting monks to live at his court as his warriors. The

Left: An etching of an ancient monk on a temple wall. Above: Some modern monks, like this man, still wear gold-colored clothing.

Ruins of a Chinese monastery provide researchers with clues to what life was like for ancient monks.

monks assured the emperor they would always help defend their country, but they wished to return to live at their temple.

Nearly a thousand years later, the Shaolin monks' fighting skills were even more famous. And the number of warrior monks at the temple had grown to more than 2,500.

During the seventeenth century, the emperor asked the Shaolin monks to go on military expeditions to border areas many times to fight off invaders and pirates. By then the monks' fighting skills had become much more combative, and they effectively used many weapons, including the spear, sword, and ax, and several small hidden weapons such as daggers and darts. Their training was difficult and their skills were legendary.

In 1674 the emperor asked the monks for their assistance, and 500 expertly trained fighting monks from the Shaolin Temple fought against a rebel army. Again the monks were successful, and the emperor invited them to live at his court as his warriors. As before, they refused and chose instead to return to their temple. This time, however, there were so many of them and they had fought so well that the emperor was afraid of their fighting abilities. He did not want to have a huge force of skilled warriors in his country that was not under his direct control. So he turned against them. In a surprise attack, the emperor's soldiers surrounded and burned the Shaolin Temple.

Many monks were killed. The rest fled to hide at other temples and in cities throughout China. They shared their kung fu knowledge and skill with others in different ways. Some of the monks became performing acrobats with the Peking Opera. Kung fu movements are even part of the traditional Chinese Lion Dance that is still performed at festivals.

A dancer performs the Chinese Lion Dance.

Above and right: A martial arts training center on the Shaolin Temple grounds draws karate practitioners from all over the world.

The temple was not totally destroyed by the fire. Many years later Buddhist monks returned to live there again. Today it is fully renovated and honors its famous history with life-sized statues of Shaolin monks in the courtyard. More than 200 sculptures show historic scenes of the monks preparing for Bodhidharma's visit, doing kung fu strengthening and conditioning exercises, sparring with each other, and fighting enemy warriors with weapons and bare hands. In the temple's Hall of White Robes hangs a large 300-year-old painting of Chinese and Indian monks practicing kung fu in pairs. Still visible today are 48 foot-shaped indentations in the ancient brick floor made by monks who stood there practicing kung fu over the past 1,500 years.

Kung fu experienced a new wave of popularity both inside and outside of China after the release of the Chinese movie *Shaolin Temple*, which was filmed in 1982. In 1986 the Songshan Shaolin Temple Wu shu (kung fu) Guild was built near the original temple. People from around the world go there to study and compete in martial arts.

3

KARATE ON OKINAWA

Three pirates with raised swords charged at the lone Okinawan fisherman. Just as the pirates got within range, the fisherman jumped and somersaulted out of their way. For the next several minutes, he dodged them. Then two more fishermen came running to help. They knew the pirates would take their boats, maybe even their lives, if they did not defeat them. The three-on-three fight was more even now. A spinning kick knocked one sword to the ground. With a few more well-placed strikes, the fishermen had disarmed the pirates.

Soon however, a dozen more pirates appeared, all holding long glistening knives. The fishermen were badly outnumbered. Fortunately for them, some neighboring farmers came to their rescue with their homemade farming tools. While one farmer used a long stick to block and strike, another twirled his threshing tools around a pirate's knife and pulled it free. Punches and kicks flew with the speed of lightning. Together, the farmers and fishermen sent the pirates running back to their ship.

Opposite page: In ancient Okinawa, only wealthy people could afford swords or knives. The poor had to rely on their own bodies for protection.

Sometimes an unarmed man had to defend himself against an attacker with a sword.

For many centuries, pirates and outlaws tried to steal anything they could from fishermen, farmers, and townspeople along the coast of Okinawa. Okinawa is now a part of Japan, but the island once was independent. Back then, most Okinawans were too poor to buy swords or knives so they used their farming tools as weapons. The Okinawan fighting style called te (tay), which means hand, was used for self-defense. Some Okinawans also learned kung fu techniques from Chinese immigrants and Buddhist missionaries living on Okinawa.

Wealthy landowners on Okinawa were the only ones who could afford swords and knives. They used them to fight each other over land. In 1478 a new king, Sho Shin, ordered a ban on weapons to end the constant fighting. His soldiers gathered up all the weapons and locked them in a warehouse near his palace. Sho Shin then made the landowners move their families into the city of Shuri, near the palace, so he could watch them. They were given jobs in Sho Shin's government, and the country was much more peaceful.

But life on Okinawa changed in 1609 when a well-armed Japanese military force invaded. The king had to quickly outfit an army to fight off the attack. However, the Okinawan forces were no match for the Japanese, who easily took over the tiny island. The Japanese again banned weapons, making it a criminal offense with severe punishment for an Okinawan to own any weapon.

Karate on Okinawa

Japan's invasion of Okinawa sent te fighters underground.

Weapons

A bo (boh) is a 6-foot stick, once used by farmers to carry across their shoulders with a basket of seeds and planting supplies hanging from each end. If attacked, the farmer slid off the baskets and was ready to fight. The bo could be turned lengthwise for blocking and the tapered ends could be used for stabbing. The bo was made of the hardest wood available so it could withstand blows from a sword.

The kama (KAH-mah) was a 3-foot pole with a curved blade attached to the end. Farmers used this razor-sharp sickle to cut rice and grass. They also found it useful when defending themselves against a sword. The pole gave them a longer reach so they didn't need to get too close to their attacker.

Nunchaku (nun-CHA-coo) originally came from Southeast Asia. They were brought to Okinawa and hidden among the farming tools during the weapons ban. They could be used for thrashing rice, but were much more effective as a weapon. Nunchaku are two hardwood sticks, 12 to 18 inches long, connected by a small rope. They are rapidly whipped to block attacks or to club the opponent. The attacker could be grabbed around the throat with the connecting rope. Nunchaku also could be used to grab the attacker's weapon and pull it away.

The sai (sigh) was a short steel tool with three prongs. It looked something like the head of a pitchfork. It may have been used originally to make rows for planting seeds, but it was more likely a weapon brought over from China and disguised as a farm tool. It worked well for trapping a sword between its prongs. The pointed ends were used for stabbing or slashing. Two sai were often used together as a pair. Or one sai was used for fighting and the second sai was tucked into the belt. If the first sai got stuck in an enemy or knocked to the ground, a second sai was handy.

The farmers also used the tonfa (TON-fah), which was the handle from a soybean or rice grinder. It was a 17-inch long stick with a 5-inch handle sticking straight out from the side. When held by the handle against the forearm it was used to block attacks. It also could be held by the handle with the long end extended out as a club. Or, two tonfa could be held together with their short handles protruding on each side.

The Japanese also outlawed te and kung fu on Okinawa, but this only made the Okinawans want to practice their martial arts even more. They secretly practiced at night in remote areas so they would not get caught. New students sometimes had to wait several years before being sworn to secrecy and then allowed to enter the training ground. Being chosen was a great honor. Other Okinawans secretly practiced at Buddhist temples on Okinawa or traveled to China to study there.

Trade between China and Okinawa had gone on for centuries and continued under Japanese rule. When Okinawans visited China, they saw demonstrations of kung fu and began to learn some of those techniques. At the same time, Chinese immigrants and Buddhist monks brought their knowledge of kung fu to Okinawa. The Okinawans added kung fu techniques to their martial art style, te, and by the eighteenth century a new style became known on Okinawa as karate. *Kara* for "China" and *te* meaning "hand." The name China hand was chosen because much of the Okinawan fighting art was influenced by the Chinese style.

——— *One's Body as a Weapon* ———

The student of karate learned that one's body provided all the weapons needed to defend oneself. The old farm tool weapons still were used when handy, but students' bodies were their first defense.

Now, as then, the fist is most often clenched in karate. The striking hand is thrust forward as the other hand pulls back to block a counterattack. As the striking fist is pushed forward, it is turned from knuckles up at the starting position to knuckles down when making contact. This twisting motion adds power to the punch, makes it faster, and forces it deeper into the target. Finger strikes, in which the first two fingers are held rigid to strike at small targets, are used to attack the eyes or throat. Or, all the fingers are bunched together like a bird's beak for striking the enemy's face or throat.

Holds, kicks, and punches were all part of an unarmed fighter's arsenal.

For fighting someone close in to the body, karate students use the heel stomp, elbow strikes, and the knee smash. Kicks, used for fighting at greater distances, include the front kick, side kicks, back kick, and the roundhouse kick. There also are many more offensive combinations and blocking techniques, which were written on scrolls and handed down from master to student.

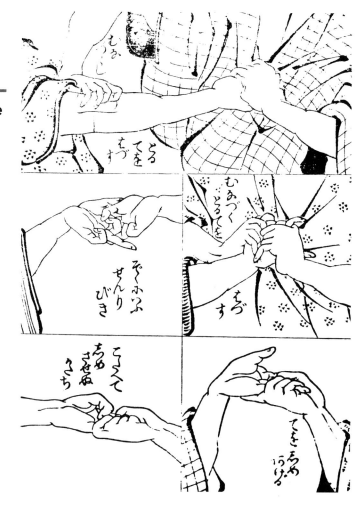

Armlocks and finger pulls were used to defend oneself.

— *Karate Moves Out in the Open* —

By the beginning of the twentieth century, karate was more openly practiced on Okinawa. But the more dangerous and deadly karate techniques were often kept secret. Sometimes a master would share these secrets with one most trusted student. Karate masters wanted to be sure that the powerful fighting skills of karate would not be used for evil purposes. The Okinawan masters felt strongly that karate should never be used in anger. They taught that karate should be used very carefully, even when defending one's life. An old Okinawan proverb states that karate and anger don't mix: "When your hand goes out, withdraw your anger; when your anger goes out, withdraw your hand."

Many karate schools, called dojos (DOE-joes), on Okinawa still follow the ancient Chinese custom of having guardian spirits. An example is a dojo with two lion statues guarding each side of the entrance. One lion is inhaling with its mouth shut tightly and the other is fiercely snarling while exhaling through its open mouth. This demonstration of ch'i breathing shows the lions' power. No evil person or spirit would want to challenge such guardians!

Some historians consider General Yi to be Korea's greatest warrior.

4

KOREAN KARATE

When archaeologists look up at the ceiling of the ancient royal Korean tomb of Muyong-Chong, they see paintings of warriors in fighting stances, punching with fists, and using the knife-hand strike. At the site of an ancient Buddhist temple, called Sok Kul An, archaeologists have found statues of warrior guards. The warriors are in karate stances with their arms in blocking positions. These artworks, evidence of an ancient empty-hand fighting style, are more than a thousand years old and were found in Korea, a peninsula on the northeastern coast of China.

In ancient times, the coast of Korea, like Okinawa, was frequently attacked by pirates. Korean warriors fought them with bows and arrows, swords, and unarmed combat techniques they called taekyon (TIE-key-on). Many of their moves were similar to the early Chinese martial art techniques, but the Koreans added their own refinement—powerful high spinning kicks—that could knock attackers off horses.

Korean-style fighters use high kicks in their fighting.

—— Academy of Fighting Arts ——

Taekyon was taught at a military academy called the Society of Hwarang-do, which means "way of flowering manhood." Boys between 16 and 20 years old who were from royal or noble families were selected to attend the academy. At this school they were taught many different subjects so they could become their country's best-educated men. They studied Buddhism, various philosophies, poetry, voice, and dance. They also were expected to be their country's greatest warriors. So their lessons in the military arts of sword fighting, archery, horseback riding, and taekyon were just as important as their other studies.

The young men were encouraged to travel and to learn about the people and regions of their country. As the warriors traveled around Korea, they performed public demonstrations of taekyon. By the eighteenth century most Koreans knew of taekyon, although taekyon techniques were taught only to the privileged.

Taekyon suddenly became more popular when Japan overtook Korea in 1909 and banned all military arts for Koreans. Instead of quitting their practices, the Koreans became more interested in martial arts than they had been in centuries. They secretly studied martial arts in remote areas like temples where no outsiders would see them.

Korea regained its independence in 1945 when Japan was defeated in World War II. In 1948 Korea split into North and South Korea. Taekyon became part of the regular training for the new South Korean military. A special commando group of South Korean soldiers, known as the Black Tigers, fought during the Korean civil war of the 1950s. As taekyon experts, they carried out spy missions in enemy territory. They were fearsome in hand-to-hand combat, but they fell easily to machine guns and tanks.

Other military units have followed the lead of South Korea's Black Tigers in learning martial arts. These Egyptian Rangers demonstrated their skills during the Persian Gulf War.

Above: Tae kwon do is a competitive sport in the United States. Right: It is included in the Olympic Games.

In 1955 most of the martial arts schools from different regions of South Korea were united into one system with the same set of rules. By 1957, the masters of the various schools agreed to name the official Korean martial art, tae kwon do. *Tae* means "foot," *kwon* means "fist," and *do* means "way." Tae kwon do translates into "way of the foot and fist." Soon tae kwon do was taught at high schools and colleges throughout South Korea.

The South Korean government then sent instructors and demonstration teams all over the world to teach their fighting art. There are tae kwon do world championship competitions held in South Korea, the United States, Europe, and South America. Tae kwon do is one of the most popular martial arts worldwide, and is practiced in more than 140 countries. It was an official demonstration sport in the 1988 and 1992 Olympic Games.

5

JAPAN'S NINJAS

Exciting tales of superhuman feats by Japan's ninjas added mystery and fantasy to martial arts lore. From the eleventh to the seventeenth centuries, ninjas worked as spies for Japan's elite warriors, the samurai. During this time, Japan was ruled by several clans, which were groups of wealthy families. Each clan had its own army. Samurai led the armies in bloody civil wars against each other.

In battle, the samurai commanded the foot soldiers from their horses. Armed with bows and arrows and their swords, the samurai dressed in armor and wore terrifying helmets with large ornaments on top. Their fearsome clothing showed their powerful status in Japanese society. If he wished, a samurai could order a person executed or a prisoner freed.

Samurai considered many tasks, like spying, to be dishonorable, so they hired ninjas to be their spies. Ninjas secretly gathered information about enemy samurai armies. Sometimes a ninja assassinated the samurai's enemies. Ninjas were feared,

Opposite page: Ninjas were feared assassins in ancient Japan.

but not respected. If caught they were tortured, then executed.

In the early days of ninjas, a ninja was loyal to one samurai clan. Ninjas risked their lives for their samurai whenever needed. They lived in wild and remote mountain areas surrounded by forests. Two areas of Japan where most of the ninja families lived were named Iga (EE-gah) and Koga (KOH-gah). Strangers did not get past the guards around these ninja villages.

Ninja Training

A child born in a ninja family would grow up to be a ninja. Class distinctions were very strict at that time. A child born in a samurai family would become a samurai, and a child born to a landowner would inherit that land. A person could not choose to be a ninja unless he or she were born into a ninja family. Ninja secrets were kept guarded among their family clan and village.

Women as well as men were ninjas. Female ninjas were called kunoichi (koon-oh-EE-chee) which means "the deadly flower." They often posed as dancers, entertainers, or servants when they were working as spies.

In 1561 Chiyome, the widow of a Japanese warlord, set up a secret school to train female ninjas. She adopted orphaned and homeless teenage girls so they could be part of her clan as ninja agents. Chiyome's neighbors all thought she was a kind and compassionate woman for taking in all these girls, but she was secretly teaching them how to spy, use disguises, relay messages, and cause confusion by planting rumors among the enemy. The girls also learned how to fight with their hands and with weapons such as the bo, knife, spear, and sword.

Training began early for children in a ninja family. They learned to run, swim, and climb as fast as they possibly could. Games most children play for fun were serious business for them. Climbing trees, pretending to be statues, balancing on beams and

Opposite page: Samurai looked impressive, but often left the dirty work to ninjas. Above: Female ninjas were called kunoichi.

branches, and playing hide-and-seek were among their lessons. By the time they were teenagers they could intentionally dislocate their joints to escape after being tied up with ropes. They would spend hours shut in small spaces or hanging from trees to build patience. They practiced leaping from tree to tree and from roof to roof, and learned the skill of silent movement. They could hide under water for hours, breathing through a hollow bamboo reed. Ninjas were strong and flexible. They could withstand the pain of an injury or cold temperatures for long periods of time. They could even go without sleep for days.

Ninja Disguises

Ninjas used many disguises in their work. They were known for their incredible "art of invisibility," which is the meaning of ninjutsu (nin-JUT-soo). They often dressed entirely in black clothing, known as the cloak of darkness, because they frequently worked at night. Black or dark brown pants, jackets, sandals, and hoods covered their whole bodies.

Ninjas also wore all white if their job took them out into snow. They wore green as camouflage when working in forests. Or ninjas would dress all in gray, so they could quickly curl up and lie perfectly still among the rocks if someone came by. Their clothes were often reversible, with each side a different color, so they could switch as needed on the job. On top, they wore an obi (OH-bee), a 9-foot cloth belt or sash, crisscrossed over their chest and back. The obi had many uses—as a climbing rope, bandage, or place to conceal weapons.

Ninjas used clothing for trickery. A ninja woman might dress up like a dancing girl to get into an enemy castle. A ninja man might dress up like a priest or carpenter. An innocent-looking townsperson who suddenly became ill and was brought into the enemy camp for help might really be a ninja. Once inside, the ninja could gather information for his or her samurai or even secretly poison an enemy.

A ninja dressed to blend in with his or her environment.

—— *Weapons out of Anything* ——

Ninjas were weapons experts. They used the bow and arrow, swords, spears, bo, nunchaku, sai, and katana (kah-TAH-nah) sword. The halberd (HALL-berd), an 8-foot staff with a blade attached to the end, was particularly useful for attacking a rider on horseback. Ninjas often hid shuriken (shoo-REE-ken) throwing blades in their obi. Shuriken are flat, star-shaped knives with three to eight points. Ninjas could throw them accurately as far as 35 feet. They carried nine shuriken because they thought that was a lucky number. They were careful not to carry four or seven, because those were unlucky numbers. The shuriken were removed from the obi and held in the left hand while the right hand rapidly fired them. Later, when firearms were invented, ninjas used those also.

In fact, ninjas were clever at making anything they could find into a weapon. They used fish nets to entangle their opponents and hid collapsible boats under bushes on the riverbank. They used climbing ropes and chains. A lady's harmless-looking fan might be a knife when folded. The sharp ends of hairpins were dipped in poison. Smoking pipes doubled as smoke bombs. The hollow scabbard or handle of a sword made a good hiding place for a blowgun and also could be used as a breathing tube for hiding under water.

Ninjas used a weapon called a caltrop, or tetsu bishi (TEH-tsoo BEE-shee), to puncture the foot of anyone following them. Tetsu bishi were first made from dried water chestnuts. Sharp pointed edges curled up around the shell as it dried. The dried water chestnuts were left on the ground for pursuers to step on. Later, iron ore was formed into balls covered with sharp points. No matter how the balls landed, spikes were always pointing up. These could puncture all the way through a shoe or sandal

Ninjas used any weapons available. If no weapons were available, they used their hands.

and injure one's foot. They also were used to protect doorways from intruders.

Spiked hand and foot bands and a tool called a shuko (SHOO-koh), or cat claw, were used to scale walls and to rake an enemy's face. Ninjas were described as black spiders crawling up castle walls. They were also known as human flies because they could climb anything and hang, silent and motionless, from a ceiling beam.

————— Ninja Chemistry —————

Ninjas learned how to prepare herbs and chemicals to use as medicines and poisons. They used herbs to heal their many injuries, and poisons from the deadly blowfish and from plants to put in their enemy's food or drinks. Darts were dipped into poison and shot through a blowgun. A musical instrument could even be used as a blowgun for shooting an enemy while seeming to be innocently playing a tune. One ninja knew an enemy went into his garden every morning to smell his fragrant flowers. The ninja dusted the enemy's roses with poisonous powder so he would inhale the poison without knowing it.

Ninjas made itching powder and laughing gas. Either of these tossed into a guard's face would distract him long enough for the ninja to sneak past. They made smoke bombs called blinders out of empty egg or nut shells filled with slow-burning explosives, fine grit, or pepper. These were flung at guards to temporarily blind them while the ninja got away. This kind of trickery caused legends to grow about ninjas' ability to disappear. One ninja used a springboard to jump over a 10-foot castle wall while making his escape. The guards chasing him didn't see the hidden springboard and thought he had actually flown over the wall.

Communication between ninjas required secret codes. To communicate from a distance, they used smoke signals and signal mirrors hidden in the woods. A particular high-flying kite might be a warning of danger or a signal that the coast was clear.

木村常陸介
伏水の城へ
しのびの
図

This early print shows a ninja, dressed in black, sneaking into a castle.

A musical tune played on a small flute could be used as a password to identify another ninja. One wrong note and the ninja would be taken for an enemy.

Sometimes their trickery, weapons, and ability to hide in shadows were not enough. They also had to know how to fight with their hands. They called their style taijutsu (tie-JUT-soo). Like most other early martial art forms, taijutsu was influenced by the Chinese martial arts. Ancient scrolls indicate that several Chinese generals fled their homeland to live in the safety of Japan's mountains when the Tang dynasty of China collapsed around A.D. 900. These Chinese warriors had been trained in kung fu and in the ways of the Buddhist monks. In Japan they quietly continued to practice their way of life and their fighting methods. They taught the original ninja mountain families their philosophy, their fighting art, and how to use natural elements to their advantage during combat.

—— Elements of Ninja Philosophy ——

The Chinese Taoist philosophy, and later the ninja philosophy, based everything on five elements: earth, water, fire, wood, and metal. These philosophies taught that the five basic elements were part of a continuing process, with no beginning and no

Ninjas were masters of breaking into houses and rooms, but—as this artwork illustrates—they were sometimes caught by guards.

end. Everything in life was seen as part of the cycle where water puts out fire, fire softens metal, metal cuts down wood, wood penetrates earth, earth dams up water, and so on. This cycle, and the balance of opposites of the yin-yang, guided their lives. The fighting style of taijutsu still uses flowing movements like the flowing, continuous cycle of nature. There are no rigid hand or foot placements for proper fighting form.

Ninjas used the five fundamental elements as the basis for their escape methods. They studied the geography of the land; learned how to swim and navigate the waterways; practiced using fire and smoke to distract, provide cover, and make explosives; used woods to hide and make medicines and poisons; and made tools and weapons out of metal.

Ninjas also used nature to their advantage in a fight. Whenever possible, they positioned their opponent to face into the sun. The ninja tried to maneuver an opponent to stand on lower ground or backed up to a tree or cliff.

Ninjas Fade Away

More peaceful times came to Japan by the seventeenth century when the country was brought under the rule of one powerful landowner, Iyeyasu Tokugawa (toh-koo-GA-wah). In times of peace, ninjas weren't needed to spy on the clans. Many ninjas went to work for Tokugawa as part of a secret police force he formed to protect himself and his family. Some of those ninjas lived and worked on his estate as his gardeners and personal bodyguards. Their pay and social status were lowered considerably. Other ninjas secretly did police work for hire while living otherwise normal lives as shop owners, clerks, or farmers. No one knew that their houses had trap doors, hidden rooms, and underground tunnels to hide in or allow their escape.

This early print shows ninjas, or perhaps assailants who only look like ninjas, attacking a household.

Over the next 200 years, many of the closely guarded secrets and techniques of ninja training were forgotten as the need for ninja services faded under new government policies. Modern Japanese culture considered ninja activities barbaric. The old ninja masters of the late nineteenth century could no longer find young people willing to devote their lives to ninja training.

Traditionally, the last living grandmaster of the clan was expected to destroy the training scrolls and manuscripts to prevent the clan's name and skills from being used by unqualified outsiders. However, some of the secret scrolls were left hidden, or were unknowingly sold off by remaining family members. Today, many ninja scrolls are on display in Japanese museums. The only authentic historical ninjutsu system still practiced in Japan has been inherited by grandmaster Masaaki Hatsumi. He was chosen and trained in the ninja secrets of that clan by its last surviving member, Takamatsu. Hatsumi has trained very few others in these secrets, only a few Japanese and one American, Stephen Hayes, who brought the art of ninjutsu to America.

American Stephen Hayes, right, is an authority on ninja lore.

Above: Ninja feats are remembered in a museum in Iga-Ueno, Japan. Left: That city also holds an annual ninja festival and parade.

6

MODERN KARATE

Gichin Funakoshi (foo-na-KO-shee) was born in the city of Shuri on the island of Okinawa in 1868. He was born prematurely, and was not expected to live long. A small and weak child, Funakoshi described himself as very shy with no confidence in himself. Fortunately for him, a school classmate was the son of a karate master, Yasutsune Azato.

Master Azato agreed to teach Funakoshi karate in his backyard. Karate still was forbidden by the government, so practices were held secretly at night. There, in Master Azato's backyard, Funakoshi practiced karate movements every night, over and over. Just before daybreak, he would sneak home carrying his lantern. His study of karate not only improved his health tremendously, but also his personality. Funakoshi believed karate changed him into a strong, energetic, and confident person.

Since Okinawa was ruled by Japan, Funakoshi's life was affected by the changes happening in Japanese government. The new government wanted all men to cut off their topknot hairdo, which was the

Opposite page: Gichin Funakoshi, an Okinawan schoolteacher, helped bring karate into the modern world.

symbol of a samurai. Funakoshi's family did not want to break its tradition and encouraged him to keep his topknot. To please his family, he left his hair in the old style. However, the government would not let him enter medical school with a top-knot, even though he had passed the entrance exams. Eventually he cut off his topknot in order to get a job as a schoolteacher. Teaching left him some free time, and he spent it all practicing karate.

Karate Becomes Legal

Military doctors, doing routine physical examinations of high school students to determine if they were fit to join the army, noticed a particularly strong and physically fit group of young men. The doctors discovered these men had been practicing karate and asked them for a demonstration. Karate had clearly made them the strongest and most fit of

Students all over the world learn karate by memorizing different katas.

all the young men these doctors had seen. Okinawan education department officials liked the results enough to permit karate in all physical education classes beginning in 1902. Karate was now legal, so Funakoshi could openly teach karate. This he did in his backyard, the way he had been taught.

As Master Funakoshi's reputation grew, young men would challenge him to fights to prove their own abilities. He never would accept these challenges because he felt there was more honor in avoiding a fight than in winning one. One of his favorite sayings tells why: "When two tigers fight, one is always injured. The other is dead." He felt karate was far too dangerous to ever use against someone. He believed the way to learn karate was to practice a pre-arranged series of moves until they were done absolutely perfectly. Such a series of maneuvers is called a kata (KAH-tah).

— Funakoshi's Reputation Grows —

Funakoshi would rather test himself against nature than against another person. During typhoons he would climb up on his slippery tiled roof and stand in the horseback stance. He held a straw mat so that when he was blown off the roof, he had something to land on. Several falls covered him in mud. Fiercely determined, he eventually held his stance on the roof in the face of the violently strong winds of the tropical storm. There he would ride out the storm all night long. This was the greatest possible physical contest for him.

When Funakoshi was 53 years old, he performed a karate demonstration for Japan's Prince Hirohito. The prince was so impressed that he invited Funakoshi to demonstrate the little-known Okinawan art of karate at an athletic exhibition in Japan. While there for the event in 1922, Funakoshi met Jigoro Kano, the founder of judo. Kano asked Funakoshi to stay in Tokyo and teach him some basic karate moves. Funakoshi felt honored by the request and remained in Japan to teach him. Soon, someone else

"When two tigers fight, one is always injured. The other is dead."

Funakoshi (second from the left in the middle row) posed with the other men who performed for Prince Hirohito in 1921.

who had seen his demonstration came to Funakoshi to ask for instruction. Funakoshi realized that if he wanted to introduce karate to the people of Japan, he would have to stay in Tokyo.

Even though Funakoshi's family had descended from the privileged class, now they had very little money. His family lived a very simple but comfortable life on Okinawa. When he decided to stay in Tokyo, he had to do so alone because he could not afford to bring his family with him. His wife remained on Okinawa with their two youngest sons, but she encouraged him in his work with karate. Funakoshi lived in a small room at a college dormitory where he worked as a janitor, gardener, and watchman. He talked the cook into taking karate lessons in exchange for a reduced price on his meals. He was allowed to use the lecture hall in the dormitory as his dojo when it was free. He even sold some of his clothes, an old derby hat and a hand-woven kimono robe, for money to meet his meager expenses.

Kenwa Mabuni, top, and Chojun Miyagi were also instrumental in introducing karate to Japan and developing different styles of karate in the 1930s.

Judo's Gentle Giant: Jigoro Kano

In the 1850s, Japan was being unified under one central government. The days of the samurai warriors were coming to an end. In 1853 American Commodore Matthew Perry arrived in Japan with several warships and a list of demands. Iyeyasu Tokugawa, the Japanese ruler, soon signed a treaty allowing the United States to trade with Japan. European countries quickly made similar treaties.

Wealthy Japanese landowners were so upset by these treaties that they forced Tokugawa to resign as head of their government and reinstated imperial rule by Emperor Matsuhito. The emperor adopted the title Meiji, meaning enlightened rule, and began to modernize Japan. This time was known as the Meiji Restoration era.

The emperor felt Japan needed to learn modern Western ways to save itself from foreign takeover. He brought in new ideas for government, technology, and industry from the West. As a modern Japanese military was established, the samurai, who had assured law, order, and stability in Japan, were no longer needed. Martial arts went out of fashion as the country modernized.

Jigoro Kano was born in 1860 during this time of change in Japan. When he was a teenager, he began to learn martial arts to improve

Jigoro Kano

his physique. He weighed only 100 pounds as a young teen. As he grew bigger and stronger, eventually adding 65 pounds of muscle, he gained confidence in himself.

All through Kano's college years, he practiced the martial art of jujutsu, the art of flexibility. Kano realized that he would need to change jujutsu from a rough and dangerous combat fighting method to a sport that emphasized health benefits for it to fit into modern Japanese society. By the time he graduated from the University of Tokyo, he had succeeded in changing jujutsu into a new sport he named judo. Judo translates into gentle or flexible way. He opened the first judo training hall in Tokyo in 1882, when he was 22 years old. He called the school the Kodokan Judo Institute.

A judo practitioner uses the attacker's own force against him or her by grabbing and throwing the attacker as he or she attacks. The attacker's own forward momentum is used to propel him or her to the mat. Jigoro Kano developed a complete system of judging and scoring judo. Locking joints, throwing, and pinning the opponent on a mat score points.

Kano traveled around the world giving judo demonstrations. At a demonstration in Russia, he threw his much bigger Russian opponent immediately after entering the ring. But before the Russian landed, Kano quickly placed his hand under the Russian's head so he would not be hurt as he hit the mat. Even though he was only 5 feet, 4 inches, Kano was known as the gentle giant.

Kano believed judo was good for women, especially for self-defense, and he taught judo to his wife and daughter. A woman first entered a formal judo class in 1893, and gradually more young women from universities and high schools learned judo in their physical education classes. Judo became the most popular sport in Japan because Kano had convinced the Japanese education department to include judo in every school by 1911. Since then, millions of Japanese have learned some judo techniques.

Judo was the first of the martial arts to come to America. The first judo training hall in the United States, located in Seattle, Washington, was established with Kano's help in 1903. President Theodore Roosevelt even took judo classes. Kano also traveled to Europe many times to help establish judo schools there.

Kano's dream was for judo to be a sport in the Olympic Games. In 1911, he became the first Japanese member of the International Olympic Committee. He promoted judo to the Olympic Committee, but it wasn't until 1964, several years after his death, that judo became a regular event in the Olympic Games.

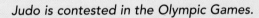

Judo is contested in the Olympic Games.

Women have always been involved in the martial arts. This drawing depicts samurai women fighting.

The Warrior's Life

Funakoshi lived his life in the manner of a true samurai warrior, following the ancient moral and ethical codes of behavior. Every day the first thing he did when he awoke was to wash himself and comb his hair until he felt it was perfect. This could take him an hour. He would then dust off his picture of the Japanese emperor that hung in his room and bow deeply to it. Then he would turn in the direction of Okinawa and bow again. Rolling up his bed mat from the floor and sweeping the floor came next. He practiced some karate katas and then had his small breakfast. He was a very humble and proper man, always faithful to samurai ways. He credited his long life, free of any illness, to karate and his simple lifestyle. He never smoked or drank alcohol, always ate sparingly, and practiced karate katas every day.

Gradually, students, including some women, from several universities around Tokyo became interested in learning karate and came to his dojo. Funakoshi welcomed women and girls to karate because he believed the benefits of karate were the same for women as for men. His wife had learned karate from watching him practice and teach on Okinawa. Office workers began coming to his dojo in Tokyo for instruction after their workday. He also was invited to give karate lessons at Japanese naval and military academies.

Classes were often conducted outdoors, the way Funakoshi himself had learned karate. When the classes clearly had outgrown the size of his dojo and yard, he shared the dojo of a fencing instructor. After he had taught karate in Japan for 14 years, his supporters raised enough money to build a dojo specifically for karate. It was completed in 1936.

Funakoshi helped create the shotokan karate katas that are still practiced today.

The ancient Japanese characters for "China hand."

The ancient Japanese characters for "empty hand."

As a youth, Funakoshi wrote poetry in Chinese and used the pen name Shoto. He chose that name, which means pine wave, because he loved walking in the forest after a strenuous karate workout and feeling the wind blow through the pine trees. His dojo was named Shotokan (SHOW-toe-kan), and his style of karate became known as shotokan karate.

Funakoshi had begun to write about karate shortly after arriving in Japan. He published books and established rules and formal requirements for advancement in karate. He was well recognized as an authority on modern karate. While a member of a karate research group at Keio University in Tokyo, he expressed his belief that karate should be translated to mean "empty hand" rather than "China hand," as it had been known on Okinawa. He explained that the Chinese letter, or ideogram, for "China" looks like the character for "empty." He felt that empty better described the fighting art because karate is done without weapons. Funakoshi also thought that karate, as he practiced it, was very different from the ancient Chinese style, kung fu. Changing the name also made karate seem more of a Japanese art than Chinese, and Funakoshi wanted to honor the country that had ruled his island home of Okinawa all his life. Funakoshi was so successful at introducing karate to Japan, that today karate is often thought of as a Japanese martial art. And Gichin Funakoshi is called one of the fathers of modern karate.

During the American occupation of Japan following World War II, Funakoshi began teaching karate to American soldiers. He even taught karate at the U.S. Air Force base in Tachikawa. American officials then asked Funakoshi to make a three-month tour of military bases in the United States to demonstrate karate to American airmen. Large numbers of Americans turned out to see his demonstrations. By the 1950s, Funakoshi felt that people in the United States and Europe were ready to learn karate. He sent his top students there to teach.

Aikido: Way of Harmony

In the late 1800s, at approximately the same time that judo was being introduced in Japan, another martial art was founded by Morihei Uyeshiba. He named it aikido (eye-KEY-doh), meaning way of harmony.

Aikido is a defensive fighting style that uses joint-locking and blocking to put the opponent off balance. The aikido fighter waits for the attack, then leads the attacker in a circular motion. The fighter redirects his or her attacker by stepping to the side or catching the attacking limb and sending him or her in another direction.

Uyeshiba was fascinated with martial arts after he learned jujutsu while a teenager. He grew to be extremely large, 195 pounds, but short, 5 feet tall. He was a soldier in the Japanese army and enjoyed the rough physical training. When he was a young man, he volunteered to settle uninhabited land on a northern island of Japan. There he lived in a log cabin, slept on a straw mat on the floor, and used a block of wood for his pillow.

Morihei Uyeshiba

Once, Uyeshiba and a priest he had met on a train went on a religious mission to Mongolia. There they came under suspicion by the government, were arrested, and sentenced to die. Japanese government authorities negotiated an arrangement to preserve their lives. Uyeshiba then went back home and taught jujutsu. He created aikido in 1926, and opened a school in Tokyo.

Uyeshiba's life of hard physical training and self-control made him a highly skilled martial artist. He could disarm his opponents so easily that it often appeared as though he had magical abilities. Aikido's techniques for subduing an opponent make it especially popular with many police departments in the United States.

7

AMERICAN KARATE PIONEERS

The ancient martial arts of Asia were first brought to the United States by American soldiers who had fought in Asia and the Pacific during World War II and the Korean War. Some began to learn martial arts in Japan and Korea while they waited to come home after the wars. The soldiers had been impressed by the way Asians could beat much larger opponents in hand-to-hand combat.

Robert Trias was one of the American soldiers serving in Asia during World War II. He was a military policeman in the U.S. Navy and the Navy's middleweight boxing champion. In 1942 he met a kung fu master who offered to teach him kung fu if Trias would teach him boxing. When the two got into the ring, Trias was unable to land a single punch on the kung fu master. He was convinced that the martial arts were worth learning.

Trias continued his study of the martial arts in Okinawa, Japan, and China. He also studied fighting styles from masters on the Hawaiian islands.

Opposite page: Jhoon Rhee was one of the first to teach tae kwon do to Americans.

When Trias returned to the United States after the war, he taught karate to the local police in Phoenix, Arizona, and opened the first American karate school there in 1946. Within two years, Trias had organized the first professional karate association in the United States. By 1955 he had organized the first American karate tournament, held in Phoenix. His organization established rules for competitions, the scoring system, officiating signals, and training guidelines for referees and judges. Robert Trias is often referred to as the father of American karate.

—— *Martial Artist of the Stars* ——

Another pioneer of American karate was Ed Parker. He grew up in Hawaii in a rough neighborhood where street fights were common. While in high school, he began to study karate and became an expert in the style Hawaiians call kenpo.

When he moved to Utah, Parker taught karate to the local police and then to teachers and students at Brigham Young University in Salt Lake City. In 1956

Ed Parker taught karate to movie stars.

he moved to Pasadena, California, where he opened a karate school. There he taught karate to many Hollywood actors, entertainers, and movie stunt performers. Parker, known as the martial artist of the stars, is best remembered for the tournament he started in 1965 called the International Karate Championships. It is still held in Long Beach, California, every August and is considered the most prestigious of all tournaments because it attracts a large number of competitors and many celebrities.

In his 60s, Jhoon Rhee still wows audiences with his board-breaking exhibitions.

— Tae Kwon Do Comes to America —

A Korean student named Jhoon Rhee came to the United States in 1957 to attend college in Texas. At a college variety show, he broke boards with tae kwon do techniques, and the board-breaking demonstration was instantly popular. Martial artists

Board breaking is flashy and grabbed the attention of American college students.

learn how to break boards without injuring themselves by practicing correct form and breathing, focusing their energy on one spot, and aiming their strike through the board. Many students wanted to learn how to develop that strength and skill, which looks impressive and is exciting to watch. Rhee had so many requests for instruction in the tae kwon do style of karate that he opened a school near campus.

For the next 30 years, Rhee taught tae kwon do at the Pentagon, the Secret Service, and to a number of U.S. Congressmen. Rhee owns five large tae kwon do schools around Washington, D.C., with affiliates in several southwestern states, the Dominican Republic, and Germany.

Rhee is well known for developing the first safe and easy-to-use protective padding. Head, hand, and foot pads are now worn in most dojos for all sparring practices and at competitions.

Jhoon Rhee's system of protective padding for students makes it possible for youngsters to learn tae kwon do without getting hurt.

HOLLYWOOD'S KARATE LEGENDS

8

In 1958 a young man from Hong Kong came to the United States to attend school. While a student at the University of Washington in Seattle, he taught his own martial art style, jeet kune do, which means "way of the intercepting fist." His name was Bruce Lee.

Bruce Lee began learning Chinese karate, or kung fu, when he was 11 years old. There were many street gangs in Hong Kong and he was involved in many fights. Shortly after he arrived in Seattle, word got out about his kung fu expertise. He was glad to give up his job as a dishwasher in a restaurant to teach his own kung fu classes. Until this time, the secrets of kung fu fighting had been taught only to Chinese and other Asian people. Lee took any student who showed an interest. He converted his garage into a gym with many training devices, some that he had designed himself. His favorites were a wooden dummy and a heavy punching bag. Fighting with a partner, or sparring, was his favorite training method because he believed it was the best test of fighting skill. He was

Opposite page: Bruce Lee, shown here in a still photo from the movie Enter the Dragon, *is the most famous martial arts movie star of all time.*

hardworking and creative, always changing and improving his techniques in his own unique style.

Lee demonstrated jeet kune do at karate tournaments. After he performed at the 1964 International Karate Tournament in Long Beach, he became well known in the martial arts community. But Lee really wanted to make movies using his martial arts skills. The performing arts were not new to him. He had been a child actor in Hong Kong when he was six years old, and his father was a comedic actor with a Hong Kong opera company.

In 1966 Lee got his first acting job, in the American television series, *The Green Hornet*. He played a newspaperman's faithful friend and bodyguard, who used martial arts to stop villains. The series lasted only one season, but Lee's character was popular with the audience.

Kung Fu in Hollywood

While Lee was trying to get a part in a movie, he taught martial arts to several Hollywood actors and screenwriters. He also did some work as a film fight coordinator, designing and arranging the movie fight scenes. During the filming of a movie, two large stunt performers were bragging about how easily they could beat the 5-foot 8-inch, 145-pound Lee in a fight, so he challenged them. Lee had them both brace themselves in any stance they chose, a few feet from a swimming pool, while each held an inflated bag in front of him for protection from Lee's kick. They did not believe that Lee could land them in the pool with one stationary kick, without any windup or running jump for added power. Lee gave one kick and the first huge stuntman was airborne above the pool. The second kick sent the other man sailing so far that he nearly flew over the pool. Neither man ever questioned Lee's ability again!

Lee's movements were so quick that his strike was often felt before it was seen. He enjoyed using his exceptional reflexes to play harmless tricks on people. One of his tricks was to remove a dime from

As Kato on the television series, The Green Hornet, *Bruce Lee brought martial arts moves into millions of homes.*

the palm of another's hand before that person could close his or her fist. Lee would rest his hand several inches above the dime in the other person's open palm. He moved and the other's palm snapped shut. The person usually would think he or she had beaten Lee, but when that person opened his or her hand, there was a nickel in it instead of a dime!

Lee's great speed and high-flying kicks earned him the nickname, the man with three legs. Another nickname was Little Dragon, because he fought with such fierceness. Those who knew Lee agree that he always pushed himself beyond his limit. The high expectations he set for himself drove him to work constantly. Everything he did became a physical exercise. He kept a punching board with him in his car so he could use it to strengthen his hands

Bruce Lee was a tireless worker when it came to martial arts techniques.

whenever he was caught in traffic or stopped at a red light. He even designed an electrical machine that he connected to his chest muscles so they could be exercised while he wrote notes on movie scripts. Bruce Lee never wasted time.

Lee regularly attended the big karate tournaments in California, and at the 1967 International Karate Tournament he met Chuck Norris. Norris had just won the title of Grand Champion by winning 13 fights in 11 hours. When the two met, Norris was simply looking forward to a good night's sleep. But the two men started talking about martial arts and before they knew it, they had stayed up all night talking and sharing techniques.

─── *Lee Makes Movies* ───

Lee got tired of waiting for a movie part from Hollywood, so in 1971 he made his first film, *The Big Boss,* in Thailand. Lee wrote, directed, and starred in the 1973 movie, *Return of the Dragon.* This movie ends with a fight scene between Lee and Norris at the Roman Colosseum.

Soon after that, Lee made his first Hollywood movie, *Enter the Dragon.* Lee plays the good guy battling a drug lord's martial arts army. Hollywood promoted the movie worldwide and Lee became an international martial arts actor. Many martial artists believe it has the best fight scenes of any movie. In *The Chinese Connection,* Lee plays a martial artist avenging the death of his teacher.

Lee was filming *Game of Death* when he died suddenly on July 20, 1973, at age 32. The movie was completed with stunt doubles and released in 1979.

Bruce Lee's son, Brandon, also made martial arts movies. This picture is from his 1992 movie, Rapid Fire. He was killed March 31, 1993, in an accident while filming The Crow.

Fifteen years later, Bruce Lee was awarded a star on the Hollywood Walk of Fame.

His death has remained a mystery of great interest to many fans. The official cause of death is listed as cerebral edema, swelling of the brain, most likely caused by a reaction between aspirin he took for a headache and painkillers he took for a back injury. However, there continue to be rumors of murder and evil spirits. The rumors of murder stem from the anger Lee caused in the Chinese martial arts community for being the first to teach its fighting secrets to non-Asians, particularly after they had told him to stop. Lee's defiance of tradition made him enemies. There never has been any proof, however, of murder.

Others feel his sudden death was the result of evil demons. The accidental death of Lee's only son, Brandon, at age 28, caused some to wonder if the demon had won against their family again. Brandon was following in his father's footsteps to become a motion picture star when he was accidentally shot in a fatal stunt accident on a movie set. Bruce Lee's life continues to interest people. Hollywood produced a movie about him in 1993 called *Dragon*.

Bruce Lee

America's Karate Star

Chuck Norris grew up in Oklahoma and California during the 1940s and 1950s. He described himself as a shy and quiet boy who was not particularly athletic. His ambition was to become a policeman. After he graduated from high school, he joined the Air Force to get experience in the military police.

He was 19 when he was stationed in Osan, Korea. To fill the long, lonely hours away from home, he joined a judo club on the base, but he soon broke his shoulder. While walking the streets of Osan one evening, he saw a karate class practicing outdoors. The students' spectacular kicks intrigued him, and he thought he could learn those kicks while his shoulder healed. He practiced five hours a day, six days a week, and became an expert in tang soo do, a style of Korean karate.

After returning home to California in 1962, he began teaching a few karate students in his backyard. Karate was still an unfamiliar sport to most Americans when he opened his first dojo later that year. By 1964 Norris was teaching karate full-time. He began entering karate tournaments to attract more students to his dojo. Two years of hard training made him a top-ranked competitor. He did so well in 1967 that he won the grand champion title at nine tournaments.

When he wasn't competing, Norris was teaching private students from Hollywood who had heard of

Chuck Norris learned karate while in the Air Force.

In An Eye for an Eye, *Chuck Norris fought against narcotics smugglers.*

his fame as a karate champion. They wanted to learn to perform karate like Norris, and he wanted to be a movie star like them. For years he took acting classes and continued to pursue his dream. He had a small role as a bodyguard in a movie in 1968, and appeared in a Bruce Lee movie, *Return of the Dragon,* in 1973. Norris began starring in action films in 1977 and has since made more than 20 movies. In 1990 he was awarded a star on the Hollywood Walk of Fame.

Norris, like Gichin Funakoshi, overcame his shyness and developed into a self-confident person through karate. He believes karate can help kids build the self-confidence they need to stay away from drugs and gangs. In 1992 he started a group, called Kick Drugs Out of America, that sponsors karate classes for sixth graders in high crime neighborhoods of Houston and Galveston, Texas. He hopes karate will help youngsters stay out of trouble and succeed in reaching their dreams.

— Martial Artists Work on Movies —

As movies with martial arts fight scenes become popular, the job of making those fights look real and exciting, yet safe to perform, becomes important. That is the job of the film fight choreographer. One of Hollywood's top film fight choreographers is Pat Johnson. He was a karate competitor when he met

Chuck Norris's Kick Drugs Out of America organization helps children and young adults learn karate.

Chuck Norris at a tournament. He also had worked as a tournament referee and had seen many fights, so he knew what made fights exciting to watch. When he moved to Los Angeles, he went to work for Norris as an instructor at one of his karate schools. He met several people from Hollywood and became a film fight choreographer. He is best known for directing

Steven Seagal is a modern-day master in Out for Justice.

the martial arts stunt work and fight scenes in the three Karate Kid movies and both Teenage Mutant Ninja Turtle films.

Jean-Claude Van Damme specializes in kick-boxing movies.

Some martial artists work as stunt doubles for actors because most actors do not do their own stunt work. The doubles, whose height, weight, and hair color match the actors', perform the dangerous and difficult maneuvers. These martial artists use their knowledge and skills to punch, fall, tumble, flip, and do all sorts of acrobatics convincingly for the camera without getting hurt. Martial artists also have worked as extras (non-speaking actors) in ninja fight scenes in the Ninja Turtle films.

Karate movies continue to be popular with audiences of all ages. Other karate masters like Steven Seagal, an aikido expert, and Jean-Claude Van Damme, a kick-boxing stylist, are well received by adult audiences. Since karate has become more and more popular with young people, Disney Studio has made less violent martial arts movies, like *The Three Ninja*.

9

KARATE TODAY

From the simple exercises of Bodhidharma, karate has evolved into a worldwide competitive sport. Every major American city has several dojos, most with classes specifically for young people. Classes may be found in community centers, gymnasiums, store fronts, and health clubs. Many different styles and combinations of styles are taught. What style is best depends on the place, the situation, and the fighter's physical size and special abilities. Very often the best karatekas (people who practice karate) learn several styles and combine the techniques.

Karatekas usually meditate before and after class to clear and calm their minds before training. During meditation, karatekas empty their minds of any thoughts of events that happened that day or of things going on around them. Being in control of the mind and body gives a feeling of inner calmness. Meditating also relaxes muscles, which improves their speed and reflexes. After the workout, meditation relaxes the body by gently slowing the heartbeat back to normal levels.

Opposite page: Karate tournaments give students a chance to demonstrate their skills.

Karatekas sharpen their sense of the space around them by closing their eyes while practicing their katas.

All martial arts make full use of all the senses. Some advanced karate classes include blindfolded sparring exercises to help students sharpen their senses of hearing, balance, and intuition. These exercises also help the student learn to sense an opponent's presence, even in the dark. Karatekas try to sharpen their sense of the space around them by closing their eyes while practicing their katas, which are a series of prearranged movements against imaginary opponents. Karatekas learn to evaluate an adversary's mood and body position so they can anticipate the opponent's moves before they are made.

Karatekas practice sensing another person's mood by concentrating on the area just outside the skin for any hint of color coming from that person. Karatekas call this color an aura and believe that it indicates the person's feelings. Blue is said to be a thoughtful color that shows the person is concentrating. Red shows anger, and yellow shows excitement, according to this theory. From this exercise, karatekas may learn to avoid possible danger by being sensitive to the feelings of people around them.

Traditions of Respect

Showing respect is an important part of karate. Karatekas are taught to bow as they enter and leave the dojo. Okinawan and Japanese dojos usually have a portrait of Bodhidharma and their dojo founder hanging on the wall, which students bow to before they enter and leave. Both before and after class the students bow to their teacher, who is called a sensei (SEN-say) in Japanese, sifu (SEE-foo) in Chinese, and sabom (SAH-bom) in Korean. They also bow to their sparring partners before and after sparring to indicate that they do not intend to hurt them. They bow to the judges at a tournament. It is proper to back away while facing the superior rather than turning away. In ancient China, the deeper the bow, the greater respect shown. If a more experienced fighter bowed first and the less

Showing respect for others, as symbolized by bows before and after sparring, is a big part of learning karate.

experienced person did not return the bow, it was considered an offense and a challenge.

Although bowing conveys respect, it has its practical side. Karate students are taught to keep their eyes on the object of the bow, supposedly to watch for a sneak attack.

Trying to Avoid a Fight

Respect also means wishing not to harm anyone or anything in nature. All martial artists agree that the best way to win a fight is to avoid it. As Gichin Funakoshi said: "To win 100 victories in 100 battles is not the highest skill. To subdue the enemy with-

The kiai helps a karateka focus his or her energy.

out fighting is the highest skill." A karateka should never start a fight and should even avoid people who are likely to want to fight, according to martial arts philosophy.

In karate, a loud yell is often added while striking or kicking. Called kiai (KEY-eye), a Japanese word meaning "spirit shout," this yell helps the karateka focus all of his or her ch'i to the area being struck. The yell can be frightening enough itself to scare off an attacker. One story tells of an old karate master who was alone in the forest when he encountered a tiger, face to face. The old man looked at the tiger and let out his loudest and most fierce yell. The tiger turned and ran into the forest to escape him!

Karate students are expected to always be clean and neat, showing that they take pride in their appearance. The traditional karate uniform or gi (ghee) is a pair of loose-fitting cotton pants and a kimono-style jacket. The gi is widest at the bottoms of the sleeves and pant legs. This design allows the cloth to make a sharp snapping sound during a forceful kick or punch.

⎯⎯ *Color of Belt Indicates Rank* ⎯⎯

A cotton belt is worn around the waist and tied with a square knot in front. The first karatekas all wore white belts. After time and many strenuous workouts, the white sashes or belts became dirty and turned a dull gray-brown, and later nearly black. Now the belt's color indicates the wearer's ability.

Jigoro Kano, the founder of judo, first used colored belts to indicate rank. He awarded the first official judo black belt in 1886. The first karate black belt was awarded by Ginchin Funakoshi in 1924. At first, the only recognized color belts were white for beginners, brown for advanced, and black for masters. Most karate schools in the United States today choose from among the colors of white, yellow, or gold for beginners; green, blue, or purple for intermediates; brown for advanced students; and black for masters.

Each rank has grades called kyu (cue). Kyu start at 10 for beginners and progress down to first kyu. When the level of black belt is reached, rank is shown according to dan, or degree, which progress upward from first dan to tenth dan. A new black belt would be referred to as first dan or first-degree black belt, then a second dan or second-degree black belt, etc. The higher dan are awarded only after many years of service to the martial arts community.

When a karateka reaches the level of black belt, he or she is then always referred to as Mr., Miss, or Mrs., regardless of age. In Asian countries, the term Master is used as an expression of respect for one who has devoted much of his or her life to mastering the techniques of a superior martial artist.

Examinations to receive each karate belt and dan must be judged by at least one black-belt instructor, and are usually conducted by a panel of several black-belt instructors. During an examination, the student demonstrates stances, punches, kicks, blocks, and combinations. Also the student must perform his or her belt-level kata and spar with one or several opponents. Finally, the student is questioned about the meaning and importance of each kata.

The term Master is used as an expression of respect for one who has mastered the techniques of a superior martial artist.

Board breaking is just one part of learning karate.

The Sport of Karate

Most people think of someone breaking a stack of boards or bricks when they think of karate. These demonstrations are done just to entertain the audience. Karatekas who do this regularly for public demonstrations have conditioned the striking area on the hand by building up thick calluses. These calluses are built up from repeated hitting on a soft board or straw-covered punching post called a makiwara (mah-kee-WAH-rah). Eventually the nerve endings in that area lose their sensitivity to pain and the skin thickens. The callused area becomes like a weapon. However, the joints near the callus eventually fuse together and become stiff and painful.

Board breaking is done by most karatekas only at belt examinations to give the students confidence in their own power.

Karate is a tournament sport today. Most cities have local tournaments for all belt levels and the best karatekas go on to compete in larger state and national tournaments. There are two different types of tournament fighting. Point karate is won on the basis of points scored for nearly making contact with the opponent. Full-contact, or knockout, karate fights are won by a knockout or by a decision of the judges. There are several worldwide karate tournaments held every year. Karatekas are trying to get karate admitted to the Olympic Games.

Many women and girls practice martial arts today. Most do it for exercise and self-defense, and some compete. The United States and many countries around the world are represented by women's tae kwon do and judo teams at the Olympics. Women also compete in all levels and styles of karate in local and international tournaments. Kathy Long has won four world championship belts in kick-boxing. To train, she spars against male opponents and runs up and down stadium stairs with weights. She also works as a stunt double in Hollywood. She performed the fight scenes for Catwoman in the movie *Batman Returns*.

Karate and Other Sports

Professional athletes from many different sports find karate training useful. They agree that karate challenges them. It teaches them to use their extra inner strength of will to go beyond their normal limits. Their karate workouts also add some variety to their regular training programs. Some major league baseball players who practice karate are Barry Bonds, David Justice, Ron Gant, and Jim Gatt.

Elvis Stojko, the 1994 World Champion men's figure skater and Olympic silver medalist, also holds karate and kung fu black belts. He uses several karate and kung fu moves in his skating routines.

Veteran basketball center Robert Parrish credits his martial arts training for his long NBA career. He says his martial arts training kept him in excellent physical and mental condition so that he was able to play professional basketball in his 40s.

Kareem Abdul-Jabbar, the 7-foot, 2-inch former Los Angeles Lakers basketball star, began studying aikido one summer when he was home from college. When he returned to the University of California at Los Angeles that fall, he met Bruce Lee and learned jeet kune do. He even appeared in a fight scene with Bruce Lee in the movie *Game of Death*. Their great difference in height and the length of Abdul-Jabbar's limbs made sparring an

Kareem Abdul-Jabbar, left, had a distinct height advantage over Bruce Lee in Game of Death.

extra challenge for Lee and interesting to watch on the screen. Abdul-Jabbar has said that he believes training in the martial arts is helpful conditioning for any sport. He has encouraged his own children to study karate. In 1989 he started an annual tournament, Kareem's Kids Karate Tournament, that raises money for needy children. The tournament draws hundreds of young competitors and martial arts celebrities.

At least 10 million people in the United States

today practice some form of martial arts. Most karatekas begin learning martial arts for self-defense. They usually find that it also boosts their self-confidence. Public schools from Texas to New York are beginning to offer martial arts classes to students. Educators hope to teach young people how to resolve conflict in the true spirit of the martial arts,

Many people all over the United States find karate a good way to stay fit.

using nonviolent ways. They believe when people are confident that they can defend themselves, they will not need to fight, and can then find a peaceful solution. Even though the martial arts have been practiced for more than a thousand years, their popularity continues to grow today.

Chuck Norris easily disables an opponent in Delta Force 2.

———— *Further Reading* ————

There are several excellent books that describe the general history and philosophy of the martial arts. The most useful to us were *The Fighting Arts* by Howard Reid and Michael Croucher (Simon and Schuster, 1983) which contains personal interviews with martial arts masters from around the world, and *Martial Arts: A Complete Illustrated History* by Michael Finn (Overlook Press, 1988). They are both fully illustrated with photos of ancient artworks, martial art masters, techniques, and weapons. Other useful and well-documented books on general karate history are *Official Karate* by David Mitchell (Stanley Paul, 1986), *Karate Training* by Robin Rielly (Charles E. Tuttle Co., 1985), and *Comprehensive Asian Fighting Arts* by Donn F. Draeger and Robert W. Smith (Kodansha International, 1980).

For information on the introduction of karate in the United States, consult *American Karate* by Don

Quine (Simon & Schuster, 1986). *Black Belt Magazine* (Rainbow Publications) is the best source of current happenings in the martial arts community and its annual special editions highlight past and present karate greats.

A fun book to read by David Chow and Richard Spangler, *Kung Fu History, Philosophy and Technique* (Unique Publications, 1980) tells several legends of Bodhidharma, details some unusual training techniques, and explains the Taoist philosophy that influenced kung fu. Zen philosophy is discussed in a book written by a sixteenth century samurai named Miyamoto Musashi, titled *The Book of Five Rings* (Bantam Books, 1982 translation). Stories of legendary karate feats are told in *The Karate Dojo* by Peter Urban (Charles E. Tuttle, 1967). Gichin Funakoshi's first book, *Karate-do Nyumon* (Kodansha International, 1988) covers karate's history and techniques.

Tae kwon do history is briefly outlined in *Tae Kwon Do* (Facts on File, 1989), by Yeon Hee Park, Yeon Hwan Park, and Jon Gerrard. Another book on this martial art, also entitled *Tae Kwon Do,* is by Mark McCarthy and George Parulski (Contemporary Books, 1984). These books are mainly concerned with tae kwon do techniques.

We found several excellent books on ninja history, lifestyle, beliefs, and weapons. Stephen Turnbull's book, *Ninja: The True Story of Japan's Secret Warrior Cult,* covers everything about the ninja and includes ninja stories, artworks, maps, and modern-day ninja festivals and ninja amusement parks in Japan. The author is an expert in Japanese studies and language, and has thoroughly researched and documented this book. In addition, Stephen Hayes, America's ninja expert, has written several outstanding books on the ninja including *Ninja Legacy of the Night Warrior* (Ohara Publications, 1985), and *The Ninja and Their Secret Fighting Art* (Charles E. Tuttle, 1981). His books give the reader a real feel for the life and times of a ninja and are illustrated with photos of ancient scrolls and weapons. Charles Daniel also wrote an interesting book about ninja fighting techniques called *Ninja Art of Unarmed Combat: Taijitsu* (Unique Publications, 1986).

The development of judo and its introduction around the world are described by Pat Harrington in the book *Judo* (Charles E. Tuttle, 1992). Her book also covers the history of women in judo. Other books with sections on judo's history are *Judo* by E. G. Bartlett (Silver Burdett Press, 1988), and *Judo— The Gentle Way* by Alan Fromm and Nicolas Soanes (Routledge and Kegan Paul, 1982).

There are several interesting autobiographies and biographies about the great karate heroes. *Karate-do: My Way of Life* by Gichin Funakoshi (Kodansha International, 1975), tells many interesting stories of his life on Okinawa and Japan. A real sense of his personality and lifestyle come through to the reader. In Chuck Norris's best-selling autobiography, *The Secret of Inner Strength: My Story* (Little Brown & Co., 1988), he shares the personal insights he gained through the practice of karate and tells how it changed his life. Kareem Abdul-Jabbar's autobiography, *Giant Steps* (Bantam Books, 1983) contains a chapter on his experience in martial arts and his friendship with Bruce Lee. The biography, *The Legendary Bruce Lee* (Ohara Publications, 1986), is a collection of articles compiled by Jack Vaughn and Mike Lee. It describes the fanatical character of Lee as a martial artist and the other aspects of his life, as an actor and family man. Other articles about Bruce and Brandon Lee are published by *Black Belt Magazine* (Rainbow Publications) and *Martial Arts Legends Magazine* (C.F.W. Enterprises). *Bruce Lee the Legend* (Paragon Films, 1984) is an entertaining and informative documentary about his life.

Winning Karate by Joseph Jennings (Contemporary Books, 1982) is an introductory book on karate covering how to select a dojo, expectations and rewards, and many techniques.

Two very useful reference books we used for spellings and pronunciations were *The Martial Arts: Traditions, History, People* (Gallery Books, 1983) and *The Overlook Martial Arts Dictionary* (Overlook Press, 1983), both by John Corcoran and Emil Farkas.

Glossary

aikido: (eye-KEE-doh) An unarmed method of self-defense founded in Tokyo by Morihei Uyeshiba in 1926 based on the principle of harmony and nonresistance to one's opponent.

bo: (boh) A wooden staff approximately 6 feet long, originally used by Okinawan farmers to balance heavy loads across their shoulders, and later used as a weapon.

Bodhidharma: (BO-dhi-dharma) The Japanese name for the founder of Zen Buddhism and the legendary founder of early karate. Known as Dharma in India and Ta Mo in Chinese.

Buddhism: (BOOD-ism) A religious doctrine originating in India.

caltrop: (CALL-trop) See **tetsu bishi**.

ch'i breathing: (chee) A Chinese word meaning "internal energy" or "life force." A deep and controlled abdominal breathing method practiced in kung fu to increase one's power. Called ki (key) in Japanese.

dan: (dan) A term that indicates the rank of a karate black belt.

dojo: (DOE-joe) A training hall where martial arts are practiced.

full-contact karate: Also known as knockout karate. A style of sparring used in some tournaments in which the competitors attempt to knock down their opponent with their strikes and kicks. A win is usually declared by a decision of the judges to prevent serious injury to the contestants.

gi: (ghee) The traditional uniform worn in karate which consists of loose-fitting, cotton pants and a kimono-style jacket.

halberd: (HALL-berd) An 8-foot staff with a blade attached to the end, particularly useful for attacking a rider on horseback.

jeet kune do: (jeet koon DOH) A martial arts style developed by Bruce Lee in the 1960s.

judo: (JOO-doh) A self-defense system and Olympic sport founded by Jigoro Kano in Tokyo in 1882. Judo uses joint-locking techniques and the opponent's strength and momentum to throw and pin down the opponent.

jujutsu: (joo-JUT-soo) The ancient unarmed combat style of the samurai and the precursor of modern judo. Also spelled jujitsu.

kama: (KAH-mah) A simple farming sickle that farmers on Okinawa converted into a weapon.

karate: (kah-RAH-tay) A martial art developed in Okinawa from a combination of Chinese kung fu and Okinawan te, later popularized by Gichin Funakoshi in Japan.

karateka: (kah-RAH-tay-kah) A karate practitioner.

kata: (KAH-tah) A series of prearranged movements against imaginary opponents. Also called "form" in English.

katana: (kah-TAH-nah) A sword with a curved blade 24 to 36 inches long.

kenpo: (KEN-poh) Hawaiian fighting style developed from Japanese and Chinese styles.

kiai: (KEY-eye) A loud yell made when making contact with the target during a strike or kick that forces the air out and maximizes body strength.

kick-boxing: The martial art of Thailand, which uses many hard kicks and punches to knock out the opponent. A win is usually declared by a decision of the judges to prevent injury to the contestants.

kshatriyas: (sha-TREE-as) Ancient warriors or warrior class from India.

kung fu: (kung-FOO) The ancient Chinese martial art that gradually evolved from Bodhidharma's The Eighteen Hands of the Lo Han exercises.

kunoichi: (koon-oh-EE-chee) The female ninjas.

kwoon: A training hall.

kyu: (cue) A rank used to designate achievement level in karate below black belt. Kyu progresses from 10th kyu to 1st kyu until the level of black belt is reached. The color of the belt worn by the karateka indicates the kyu.

makiwara: (mah-kee-WAH-rah) A straw-covered striking post or mat used in karate to strengthen the striking area of the body by repeatedly hitting or kicking.

martial arts: A general term for the Asian fighting arts.

ninja: (nin-JUH) Secret warriors in ancient Japan. They were known for their cunning and daring.

ninjutsu: (nin-JUT-soo) The Japanese term for the art of invisibility, which ninjas were known for because they were skillful at blending into their surroundings.

nunchaku: (nun-CHA-coo) Two hardwood sticks connected by a short rope used by Okinawan farmers to thrash rice and as a weapon. When swung rapidly, they can strike with great force, and the rope can be used to grab the opponent or his weapon.

obi: (OH-bee) A 9-foot cloth belt or sash worn by a ninja, crisscrossed over the chest and back. An obi was used as a climbing rope, bandage, and hiding or carrying place for their weapons. Modern karatekas wear a colored obi, which shows their level of achievement in the martial art.

point karate: A karate competition judged on the basis of the number of points scored by competitors for making light contact with the opponent.

sabom: (SAH-bom) A Korean term for "teacher."

sai: (sigh) A small steel weapon with three prongs like the head of a pitchfork. Probably a weapon smuggled over to Okinawa from China during the weapons ban and hidden among the farming tools. It was particularly useful for trapping a sword between its prongs.

samurai: (SAM-uh-rye) The warrior swordsmen of feudal Japan.

sensei: (SEN-say) A Japanese term for "teacher."

shotokan: (SHOW-toe-kan) The Japanese form of karate taught by Gichin Funakoshi.

Former martial arts champion David Bradley in American Ninja 3.

shuko: (SHOO-koh) A weapon used by ninjas. A metal band that slips over the hand with spikes extending from the palm used for climbing or for scraping an enemy's face. Also called a cat claw.

shuriken: (shoo-REE-ken) A throwing blade with three to eight sharp points.

sifu: (SEE-foo) A Chinese term for "instructor."

tae kwon do: (TIE-kwon-doh) The Korean version of karate, which uses high kicks.

taekyon: (TIE-key-on) The ancient Korean martial art that tae kwon do is based on.

taijutsu: (tie-JUT-soo) The ninja style of fighting that uses natural, flowing movements.

tang soo do: (tang soo DOH) A Korean martial art, slightly different from tae kwon do.

Taoism: (DOW-ism) An ancient Chinese philosophy developed by the scholar Lao Tzu in the sixth century B.C. that teaches living in harmony with nature and understanding the balance of opposites in the universe.

te: (tay) The Okinawan fighting style that was combined with Chinese kung fu to become karate.

tonfa: (TON-fah) The handle on a rice or soybean grinder that the Okinawan farmers used like a club.

tetsu bishi: (TEH-tsoo BEE-shee) A rounded ball with sharp points protruding from all sides. Ninjas would leave them on the ground to injure pursuers who stepped on them.

vajramushti: (vah-ra-MOOS-ty) An ancient Indian fighting art from as early as 1,000 B.C.

wu shu: (woo SHOE) The Chinese word for the fighting style known as kung fu in the United States.

yin-yang: The Chinese theory that everything in the universe is a balance of opposites, passive and active.

Zen Buddhism: The branch of Buddhism founded by the Indian monk, Bodhidharma, in the sixth century. Also known as Chan Buddhism in China.

Photo and Illustration Acknowledgments

Photographs are reproduced with permission of: pp. 6, 42, American Tae Kwon Do Association; pp. 8, 12, 13, 15, 16, 17, 18, 23, 25, 26, 27 (both), 30, 31, © Dennis Cox/China Stock; pp. 9, 64, 95, 96, Luana Metil; p. 10, Asian Art Museum of San Francisco, The Avery Brundage Collection (B60J962); p. 14, Freer Gallery Smithsonian Institution, Washington, D.C. (02.228); p. 20, British Museum; pp. 21, 37 (bottom), Karate Profiles Made In America; pp. 22, 28, Carl Wilcox; p. 29, Singapore Ministry of Culture; pp. 32, 34, 36, 39, 40, 48, 50, 51, 56, 57, 58, 59, 61 (both), 70, Stephen Turnbull/Japan Archive; p. 35, International Society for Educational Information; p. 37 (top), © Sue Vanderbilt/Unicorn Stock Photos; p. 41, Nik Wheeler, Aramco World; pp. 46, 99, Unicorn Stock Photos; pp. 78, 79, 92, © Dick Young/Unicorn Stock Photos; p. 98, Joseph L. Fontenot/Unicorn Stock Photos; pp. 102-103, © Eric R. Berndt/Unicorn Stock Photos; p. 44, Korean National Tourism Corporation; p. 45, Department of Defense; p. 47, © Shaun Botterill/Allsport; pp. 53, 54, 60, Stephen K. Hayes/Nine Gates; pp. 52, 80, 82, 83, 84, 87, 88, 90, 91, 101, 104, 109, 111, Hollywood Book and Poster; p. 62, Courtesy of David Palumbo; p. 66, International Karate Research Society; p. 67 (top), Courtesy of Rudy Crosswell; p. 67 (bottom), Courtesy of Morio Higaonna Sensei; p. 68, Courtesy of United States Judo; p. 69, Constance H. Halporn/United States Judo; p. 71 (both), Amateur Athletic Union; p. 73, United States Aikido Federation; pp. 74, 77, Jhoon Rhee Foundation; p. 76, International Kenpo Karate Association; pp. 85, 86, Photofest; p. 89, Monica Hall/Kick Drugs Out of America Foundation.

Map on pages 2-3 by Laura Westlund. Calligraphy on page 72 by Kenichi Tazawa. The Stephen Turnbull photographs appear courtesy of Firebird Books, London, Publishers of Turnbull's book, *Ninja: The True Story of Japan's Warrior Cult,* and its United States distributor, Sterling Publishing. The Luana Metil photographs appear courtesy of the Twin Cities Martial Arts Center (Edina, Minn.).

Front cover photographs from © Dennis Cox/China Stock and Hollywood Book and Poster. Back cover photographs from © Dennis Cox/China Stock and Karate Profiles Made In America.

Index

Jean-Claude Van Damme demonstrates his kick-boxing prowess in numerous movies.